chaos interrupted

Dawn Thomas-Cameron

BookLeaf Publishing

Presentation by *BookLeaf Publishing*

Web: www.bookleafpub.com

E-mail: info@bookleafpub.com

ISBN: 9789357617956

First edition 2023

DEDICATION

To my kids. Chaos embodied.

introduction

Dawn
creative inspired
don't look too deep
depressed alone
self

magick

Magick
Omnipresent
Flows Thru Nature
One only needs to
Look...

ode to (clear) communication

Communicate clearly with whom...
Do not assume
that your meaning
comes through gleaning

Enunciate within your mind
Detail behind
Meaning portrayed
An awkward way

Ensure work need not be redone
Omit doubt that one
Need not guess at
And then come flat.

aqua

Pure liquid
Surrounding my body
Relaxation
Floating in luxury

Steam rises
    (Evaporating water)
Vapour condenses around particulates.
Suspended to the threshold.

Where it falls back to Earth
    as rain, sleet, ice, snow
    (precipitation)
Pooling, flowing, rushing, sparkling
Pure liquid.

energy

Energy
  bubbling forth
   h o p p i n g
             like a bunny

   grrrr-owl-ing
             like a lion

  s
    l   ri
     i e n
      th   g
             like a snake

  b u c n
   o n i g
             like a monkey

TRUMPETING
             like an elephant

pounding
             like horse hooves

never ending
always moving
sometimes pausing

to start again

(children)

luck

Is luck somehow dependent on a person or
circumstance?
A set of confluences?
Tied to a soul or being?
Is it reciprocated?
Karma in, karma out?
A flip of the dice in the game of life?
Why is one lucky and one not?

spring

buds start to blossom
    though it's cold
new life from a frozen wasteland
    brings birds chirping
      if you listen
squirrels dashing up and down
green leaves form
    despite lack of rain

nature is amazing

villain

Evil
    Maniacal psychopath
    Do you wanna know
        how I got these scars?
Joker

f*ck me

Homeschooling and working
    do NOT go hand in hand
I need help;
    do this for me,
    watch me,
    wipe my bum
       (yelled out during a work meeting).
Crying for no reason
    alligator tears;
    not willing to participate;
    no motivation.
Nagging,
    and nagging,
      and nagging.
Just do your goddamn work!

peace

I'm awaiting peace
   when the house is quiet
And then the neighbour's dog barks
Or car music pounds
Or doors slam.
Never a moment of peace.

change

Change is bound to
Happen
And
Not being prepared is a
Grievous
Error.

Ordinary people
Ran to the store.

Demonstrating lack of restraint
Over the purchase of
Nothing more than

'Toilet paper, sanitizer, and Lysol wipes.'

Chaos
Has
A
Natural tendency to
Gift people with
Egotism.

bear

Grumpy
　　Grizzly
　　　　Leave me alone
Mama bear

untouchable

Tempus est umbra in mente

a human concept we hold ourselves to
a construct in which to bound our memories
abstract in definition
     fleeting
flying by with enjoyable moments
dragging by when awaiting something
priceless
wasted

time is a shadow of the mind

a blitz poem

leaves free floating
leaves piled up
up to three feet
up to jump inside
inside the out
inside imagination
imagination run amuck
imagination unleashed
unleashed dog
unleashed ideas
ideas to write
ideas to create
create some art
create a painting
painting my house
painting a glass
glass balls hanging
glass shattered
shattered dreams
shattered connections
connections to nature
connections to neurons
neurons fire
neurons are a concept
concept like time

concept of money
money is freeing
money buys happiness
happiness is an illusion
happiness is dopamine
dopamine is a drug
dopamine lack is depression
depression sucks life
depression is lonely
lonely people cry
lonely is quiet
quiet is mindfulness
quiet is peace
peace can be real
peace on earth
earth rotates
earth is sick
sick like me
sick needs healing
healing hurts
healing power
power reigns supreme
power consumes
consumes life
supreme nothingness

crazy cat lady

ears   mew

perk up   mrrrowww

listening to keyboard clacking;

curious; murder mittens;

nudges hand waiting to be pet;

affectionate fur ball; mischievous eyes;

settles atop sofa back; legs tucked under;

eyes slightly closed; elongated; intrusive;

"football player" and "princess kitty";

white whiskers twitching; serpentine tail

swishes; playful and inquisitive; trouble;

affectionate; purring contentedly;

content to just be; startled

=> sprints away;

skittish

ode to my 1965 ford fairlane

Two door hardtop; colour gray
Actual keys back in the day
Power nothing; "armstrong steering"
Gleaming chrome; people leering

Built to last, a metal tank
Once hit a pole and nothing sank
Forty below and not plugged in
Engine would still start and spin

Gas put in under back plate
For parts, we simply had to wait
$200 per year, plate and insurance
$20 to fill; lots of endurance

little ones

Ingredients

1 child
1 cup spunk
2 cups energy
1/2 tsp attention span
4 cups mud
10 dead grasshoppers
1 ball

Directions

1. Must be done outside.
2. Mix together energy, spunk, and attention
plan.
3. Dump in mud and grasshoppers. Stir well.
4. Pour over the ball—the more mess, the better.
5. Bounce the ball all around the area.
6. Let the child rest a couple hours.
7. Throw the child in the bath to clean for
another day.

Substitutes (for step 3 and 4):
- swimsuit, water, water containers
- legos, imagination
- colourful stones, sand, strainer, water
- rocks, paint, paint brushes

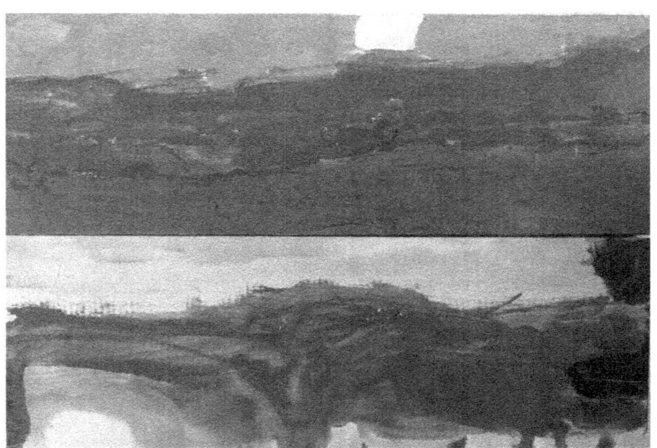

idiocrasy

people are getting dumber by the day

YouTube videos of people playing games
    yelling and dictating play by play
Why?

Drivers controlling hurtling hunks of metal
    high speeds, unaware of others
    ignoring others
    cutting other cars off
    stopping in merge lanes
PAY ATTENTION

Ridiculous labels
    do not put child in washer
    coffee is hot
    peanut butter contains peanuts
    water is wet
    do not use disinfectant wipes on babies
Remove labels, let Darwin's law take out
stupidity.

Dumbass trends
    eating tide pods
    ice water challenge
    pranking your friends

shaking head

Idiocrasy indeed.

if...

if we could attain world peace
by sacrificing x number of people
  each year,
how high would x be to be acceptable?

consider the number of lives war takes,
  starvation, disease, suicide,
  auto accidents, murder

if all this was gone,
if we could live in absolute peace,
if everyone could be equal in society

how low would x be to be acceptable?

get crazy!

What is your definition of normal?
Is it casual or something formal?
Is it (simple?) mental deviation
   or does it become from oration?
Crazy is as crazy does as they say,
   but who is to define it anyway?
If everyone jumps off a make-believe bridge,
   does that dictate you too spring from that
   edge?
If you talk to yourself or passed loved ones,
   it's okay; you're allowed out in the sun.
Sing out loud; dance around; wear what you
want.
This in itself does not make you savant.
Life is much too short to play by the rules;
   crack a smile; make a face; just do not drool.

organized chaos

25

Pick up something to write with -

pencil

Scratch thoughts out messily -

fragments

Or written ever so neatly -

pattern

Thought swirl from mind to paper -

bearing

The possibilities are endless -

witness

www.ingramcontent.com/pod-product-compliance
Lightning Source LLC
Chambersburg PA
CBHW070732160726
48003CB00006BA/2462